"Anything we don't like, we'll turn it into a happy little tree or something; we don't make mistakes, we just have happy accidents."

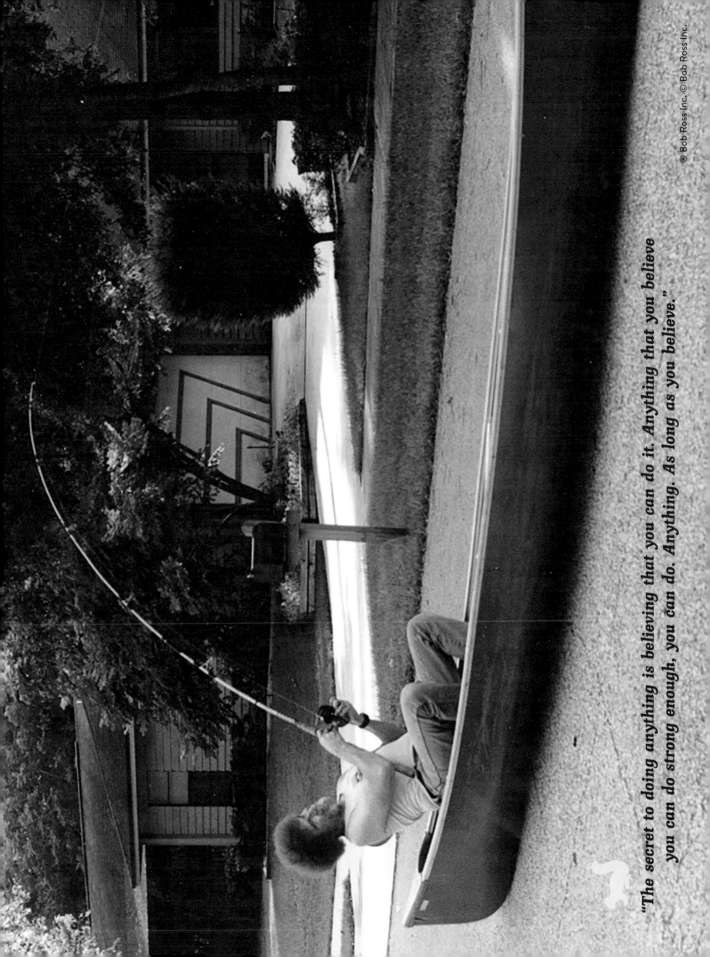

"The secret to doing anything is believing that you can do it. Anything that you believe you can do strong enough, you can do. Anything. As long as you believe."

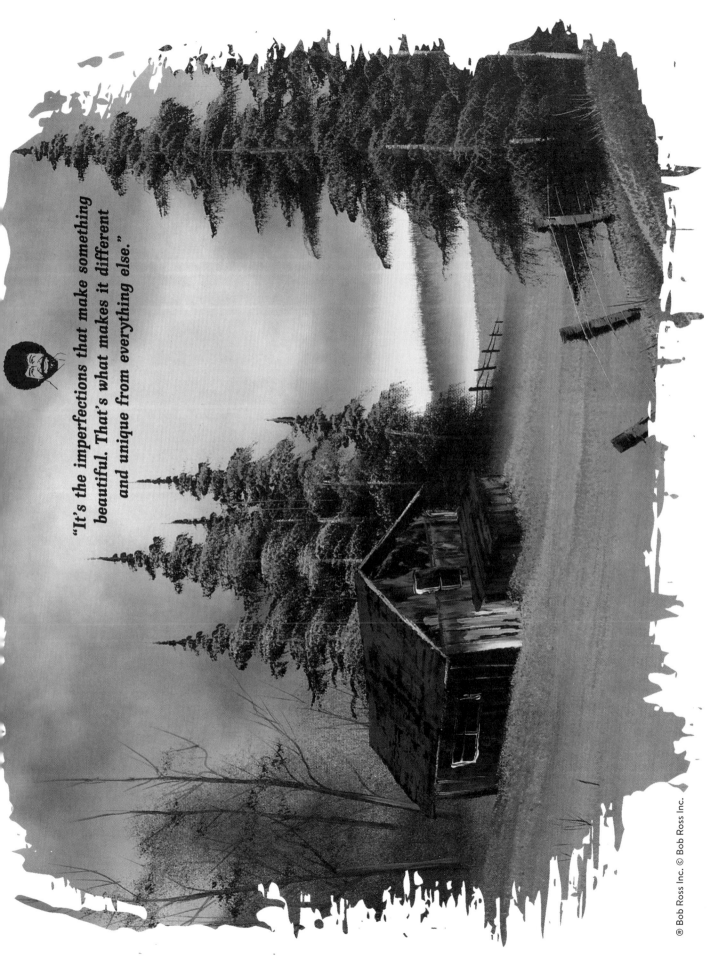

"It's the imperfections that make something beautiful. That's what makes it different and unique from everything else."

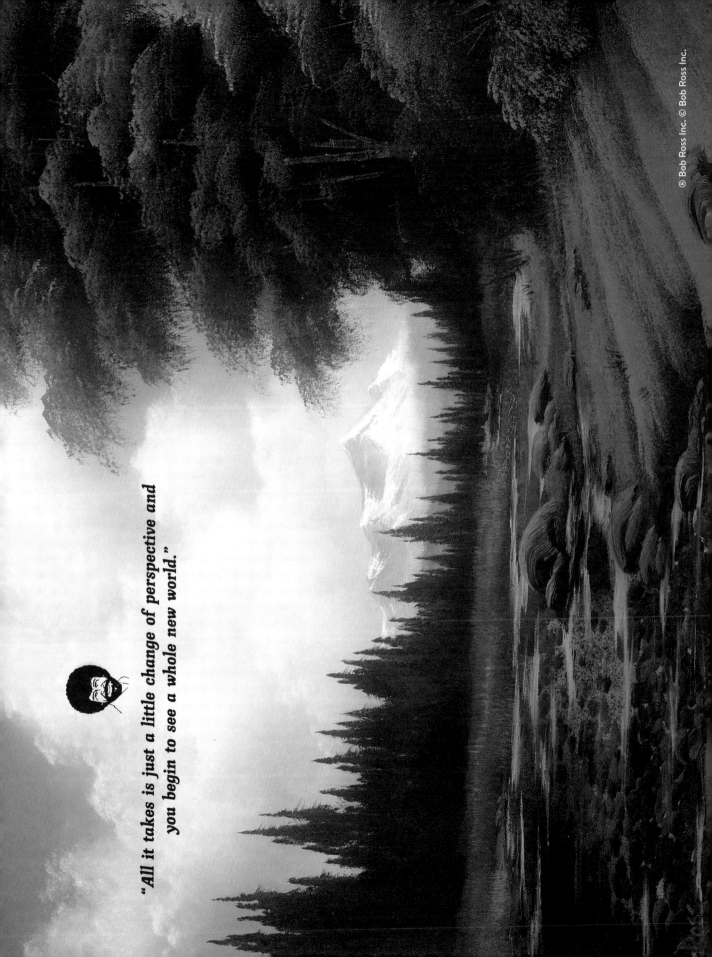

"All it takes is just a little change of perspective and you begin to see a whole new world."

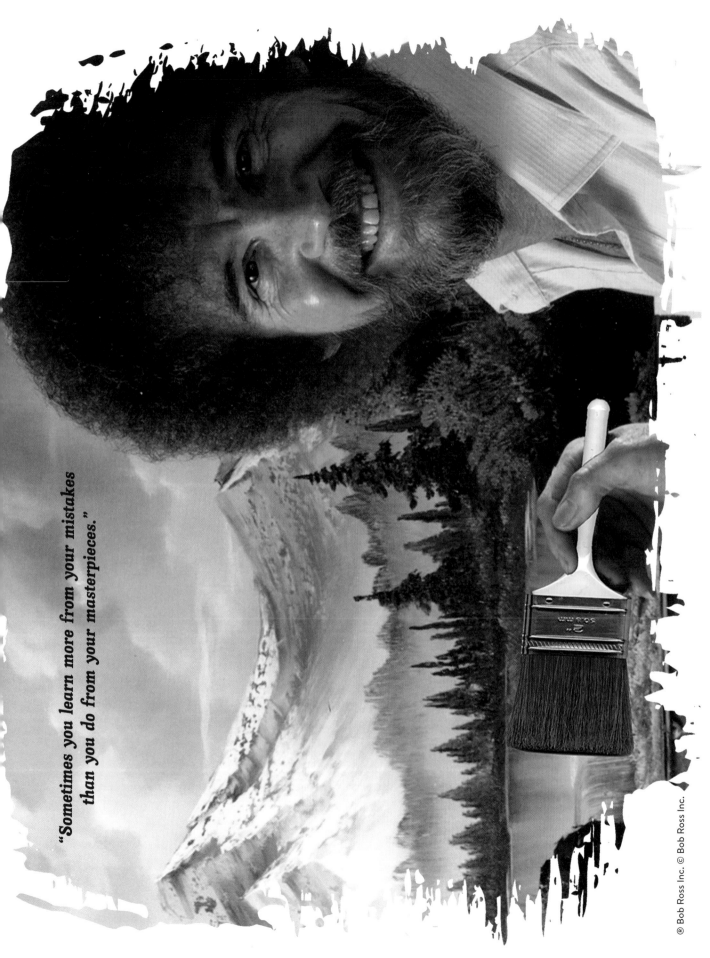

"Sometimes you learn more from your mistakes than you do from your masterpieces."

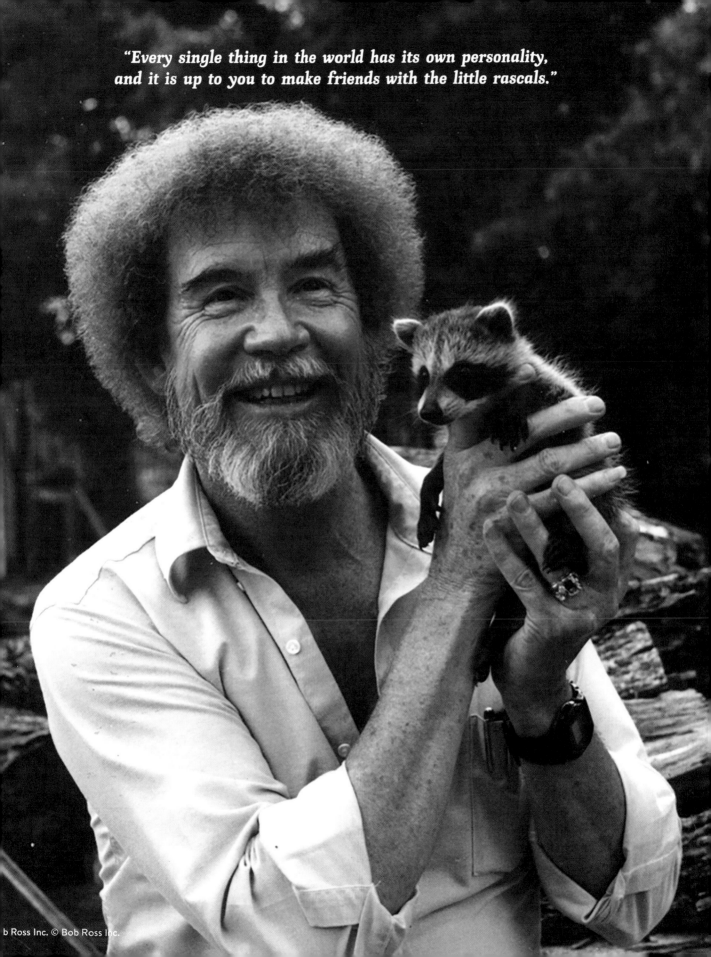

"Every single thing in the world has its own personality, and it is up to you to make friends with the little rascals."

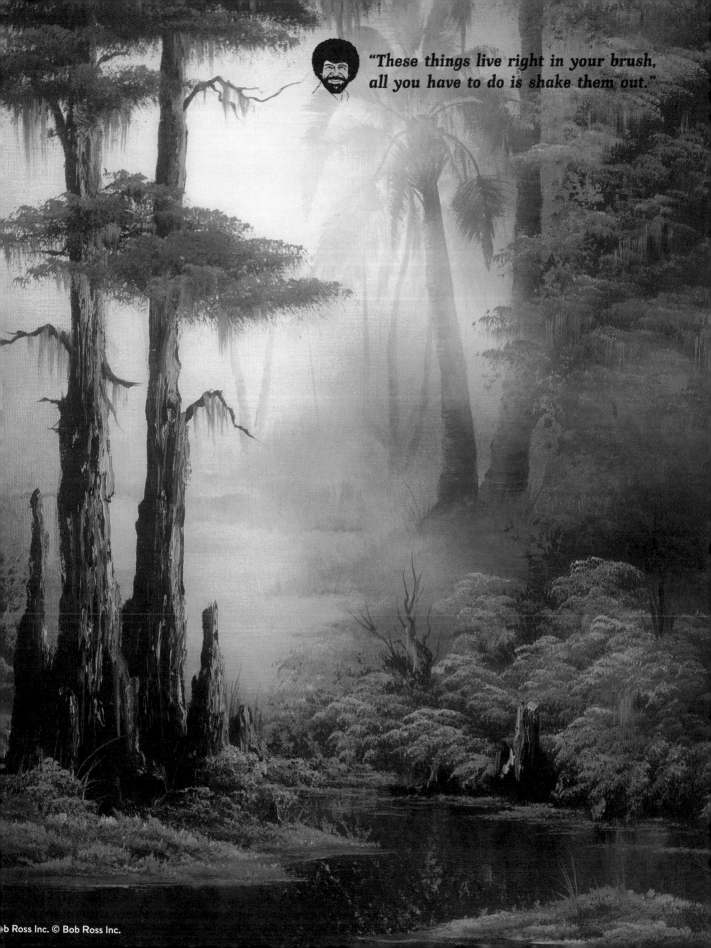

"*These things live right in your brush, all you have to do is shake them out.*"

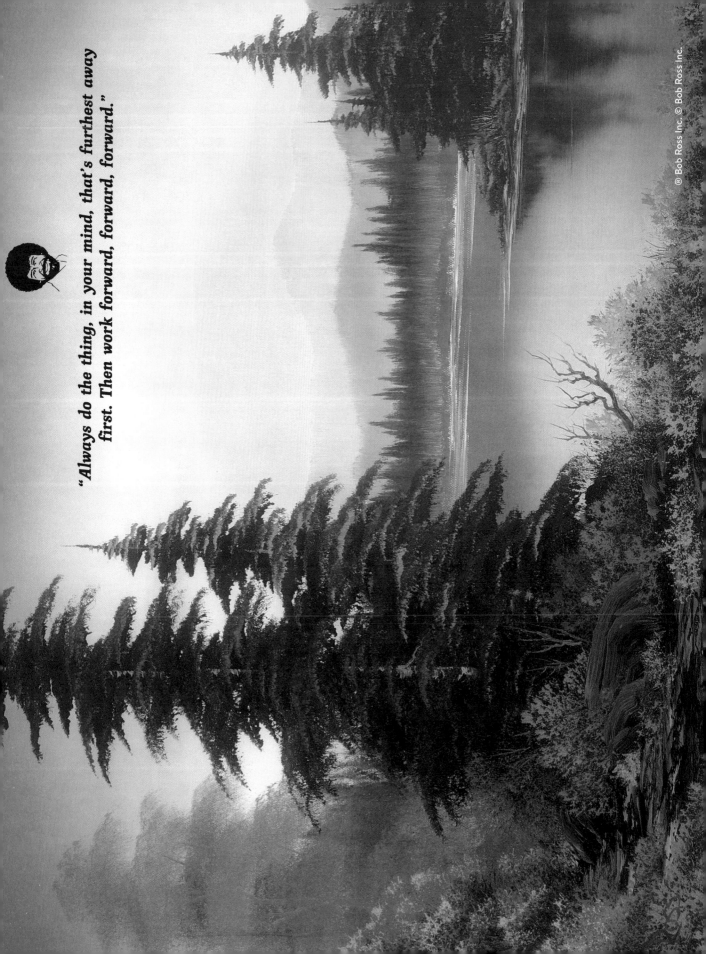

"*Always do the thing, in your mind, that's furthest away first. Then work forward, forward, forward.*"

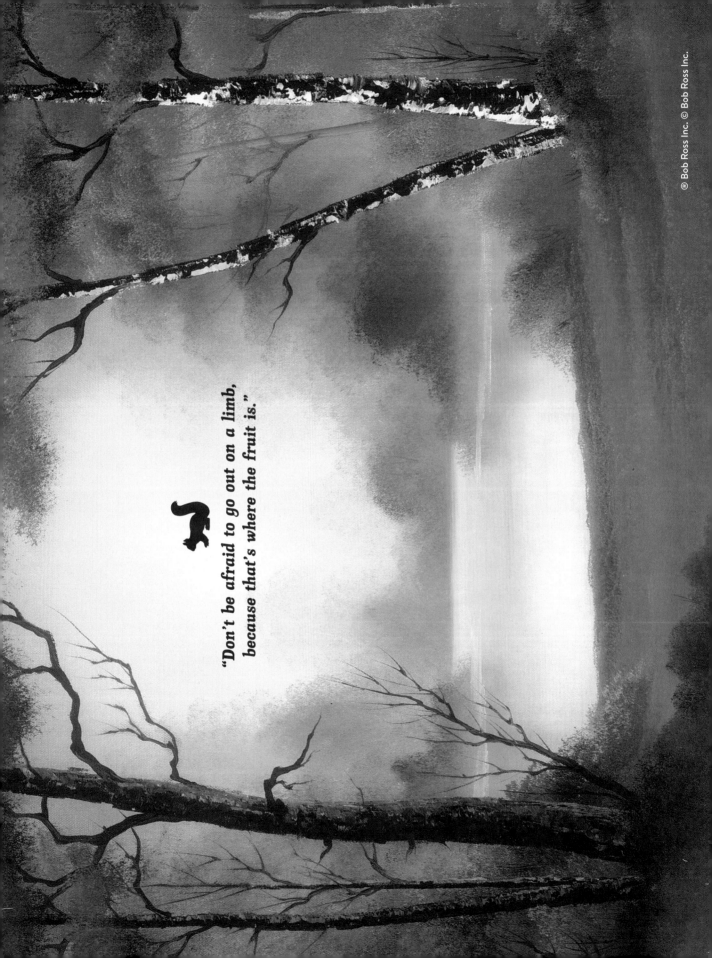

"Don't be afraid to go out on a limb, because that's where the fruit is."

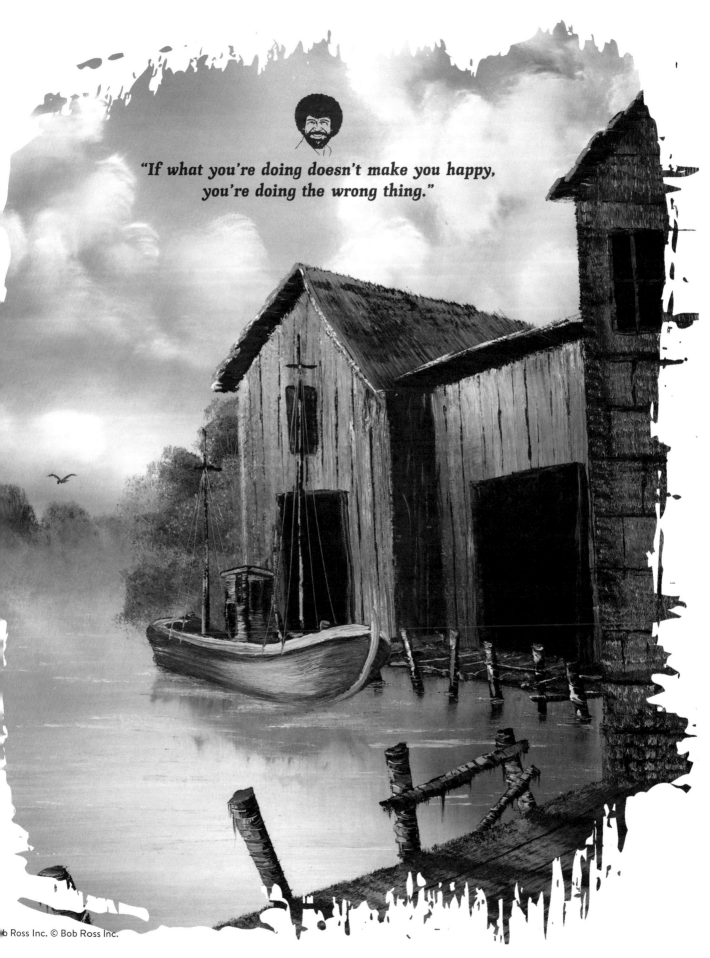

"If what you're doing doesn't make you happy,
you're doing the wrong thing."

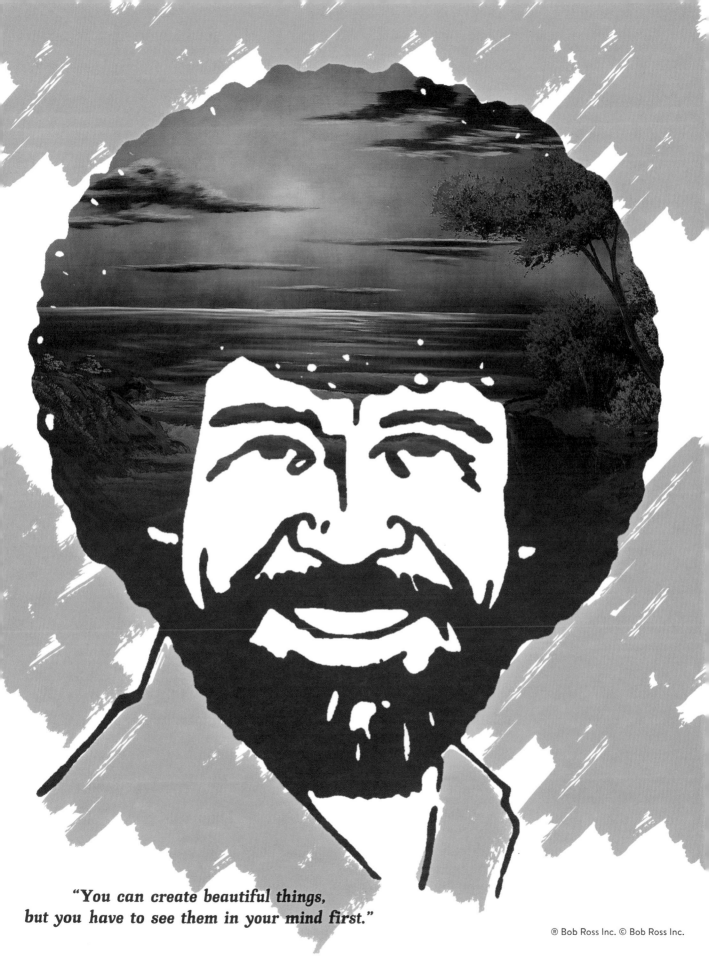

"You can create beautiful things, but you have to see them in your mind first."

® Bob Ross Inc. © Bob Ross Inc.

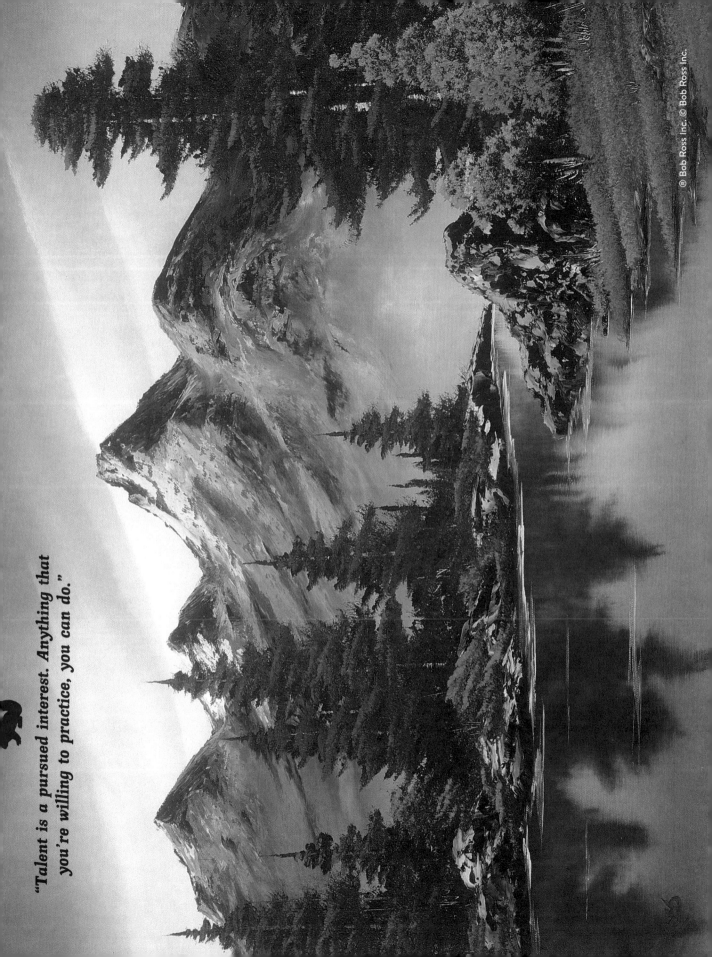

"Talent is a pursued interest. Anything that you're willing to practice, you can do."